PRAYING
&
GETTING RESULTS

PRAYING
&
GETTING RESULTS

BOB GASS

All scriptures are taken from the King James Version unless otherwise noted.

Other Bible Translations used as noted:

TM - The Message
NIV - New International Version
NLT - New Living Translation
LB - Living Bible
AMP - Amplified Bible
NKJV - New King James Version

PRAYING AND GETTING RESULTS
ISBN 0-88270-870-8
Copyright ©2001 by Bob Gass Ministries
P.O. Box 767550
Roswell, GA 30076

TABLE OF CONTENTS

PREFACE

Growing up, much of what I heard about prayer either left me under a truckload of guilt or wore me out with pious sounding clichés.

Because I couldn't spend two or three grueling hours a day on my knees, or weave several scriptures into each prayer, or move mountains, I felt like a failure.

Then I discovered these wonderful words: "If we ask anything according to his will, he hears us. And if we know that he hears us - whatever we ask - we know that we have what we asked of him" (1Jn 5:14-15 NIV).

No secret-code talk or public displays of piety there; just one condition - pray according to God's will, which is revealed in His Word or through the inner-impressions of His Spirit.

Once I understood that, praying became natural,

comfortable, and even exciting. For now I could pray and get results, and you can too!

That's what this book is all about!

ACKNOWLEDGEMENTS

Some of the prayers found in the last chapter of this book are taken from the writings of T. D. Jakes and his wonderful *Woman Thou Art Loosed* edition of the Bible. (*Nelson Publishers*).

1

MAKE IT A HABIT

We keep doing *only* the things that reward us! So when prayer becomes an unrewarding experience - we quit - and then we feel guilty.

If that's where you are today, you're not alone. We all go through this on our way to discovering that it's not about kneeling positions, pious words, stopwatches, and prayer lists. It's about a relationship! It's about having regular conversations with your Father!

I began coming to Him quicker, staying in His presence longer, and enjoying it more, when it dawned on me that He loved me unconditionally, forgave me each time I asked Him, and wanted nothing but the best for me.

It's like a good marriage. You don't hold anything back, and you don't try to manipulate the other person. But you have to work at it. Good relationships don't happen in a few fleeting, mechanical moments, nor can they be built on an emergency-basis either.

E.M. Bounds writes, "God's acquaintance is not made hurriedly. He doesn't bestow His gifts on the casual or hasty comer and goer. *Spending time with Him* is the secret to knowing Him, and having influence with Him."

Everything in my life seems to conspire to keep me from the place of prayer. When that happens, it shows up in different areas.

"Why is it such a battle?" you ask. Because the place of prayer is where you meet with God to be instructed ... corrected ... cleansed ... loved ... built up ... and prepared for your future. It can be *anywhere*, but it must be *somewhere*! It can be *any time*, but it must be a *set time*! For me it had to become the most important appointment in my day.

Jesus is our example. He rose before daybreak to pray because He knew what was waiting for Him. (See Mark 1:35). He made deposits in the morning, so that He could make withdrawals the rest of the day.

Without time spent in prayer *what* do you have to draw on? You'll work harder and accomplish less because you're operating in your own strength. But after you've prayed, you'll struggle less and accomplish more because you're operating in His strength.

Personally, my challenge is in getting so involved with the *work* of the Lord that I finish up neglecting the *Lord* of the work. Paul knew how easy that was, so he prayed, "I want to know Christ" (Php 3:10 NIV). The Amplified Bible says, "That I may progressively become more deeply and intimately acquainted with Him." Nothing can be born until it's first conceived. Nothing can be conceived until there's first an act of intimacy between two people. And there can be no intimacy unless there's first a *desire*.

That means setting aside time each day to spend with God, and disciplining yourself to keep it. If you're diligent about keeping other appointments, but feel that you can *change* or *cancel* your appointment with Him anytime you want to, can you imagine how that makes Him feel? Be careful; God's Spirit can be grieved.

"But I'm so busy," you say. That's about the lamest excuse you can offer. How you spend your time reveals what's important to you. If you don't pray, it's either because you don't realize its potential or you're not aware of how much you need God's help. Change your schedule! Rearrange your priorities! Make time for prayer! Because you won't succeed, as God counts success, until you do.

Martin Luther once said, "I have so much business today that I'll never get it done unless I spend the first part of my day in prayer." John Wesley, founder of the Methodist Church, said, "God does nothing except in answer to prayer." It's not optional. If you want to see *anything* of lasting worth accomplished, you must pray, and pray with confidence.

When you think about it, every failure is, in essence, a prayer failure! If you don't pray, the best thing that can happen - is nothing. You see prayer puts the situation into God's hands, otherwise, whose hands is it in?

But it's useless to pray if you (a) have no faith that God will answer; (b) have no confidence because you feel unworthy to stand before Him; (c) think that prayer is about the right words, the right feeling, the right posture, or the right length of time.

Sometimes we say, "I'll remember that in my prayer time." Yet the Bible says, "Pray without ceasing" (1Th 5:17). The truth is you can pray anywhere, any time, and about anything. Your prayers can be verbal or silent, long or short, public or private. The words "pray without ceasing" just mean - be in conscious contact with God at all times.

"But I don't feel like my prayers are good enough to get an answer," you say.

Then, there are two things you need to know: *First*, the Holy Spirit helps you in prayer. Listen, "He does our praying in and for us ... and keeps us present before God" (Ro 8:26-27 TM). *Second*, Jesus stands continually before God on your behalf. Listen again, "He's always on the job to speak up for [us]" (Heb 7:25 TM).

Now if two out of the three Persons in the Godhead are working for you, surely the most imperfect prayer will be perfect by the time it reaches the Throne of God! Knowing that should take the pressure off and help you to develop confidence in simple, believing prayer.

Does your prayer life need a tune-up? To find the answer, I've learned to ask myself these three questions:

1. How's my consistency? If you can't remember when you last took time to pray, you need to do something about it. Without prayer you're undirected and unprotected.

2. How's my sincerity? More liturgy than life?

Daily, but dull and dry? That's because you don't know enough about who you're talking to, or how He feels about you. The truth is, as you get to know Him better, you'll want to spend more and more time with Him.

3. *How's my faith?* Do you sometimes wonder if prayer really changes anything? Or why on earth a God in heaven would want to talk to you or hear anything you have to say? After all, if He already knows everything, what can you tell Him? And if He decides everything, why even bother?

Here's the score: prayer is not for God's benefit, it's for *yours*! Where else can you go to bare your soul without fear, and walk away cleansed, comforted, counseled, and corrected?

Your prayers work not because of how well you say them - but because of how well He *hears* them. You don't have to understand prayer to enjoy its benefits anymore than you have to understand the law of aerodynamics in order to fly. Just pray! Get on the plane and trust the pilot to take you where you need to go.

Max Lucado says, "Forget about the wrapping; just give the gift. It's better to pray awkwardly, than not at all." Listen, "He will call upon me, and I will answer him" (Ps 91:15 NIV). There it is in black and white - God's invitation to ask, and His promise to answer. What more do you need?

2

BELIEVE YE THAT I AM ABLE TO DO THIS?

"**A**nd when Jesus had departed thence, two blind men followed him, crying, and saying, Thou Son of David, have mercy on us. And when he was come into the house, the blind men came to him: and Jesus saith unto them, *Believe ye that I am able to do this?* They said unto him, Yea, Lord. Then touched he their eyes, saying, According to your faith be it unto you. And their eyes were opened" (Mt 9:27-30).

Shortly after Dallas Theological Seminary was founded in 1924, it almost went bankrupt. Its creditors were ready to foreclose at noon on a particular day. That morning Dr. Harry Ironside and the founders of the school met in the President's office to pray for a miracle. Ironside prayed, "Lord, we know that the cattle on a thousand hills are yours. Please sell some of them and send us the money."

Just about that time a tall Texan in boots and an open-neck shirt strolled into the business office. "Howdy!" He said to the secretary. "I just sold two trainloads of cattle over in Fort Worth, and I feel God wants me to give the money to the seminary. I don't know if you need it or not, but here's the check."

The secretary, who was aware of the crisis, took it and knocked on the door of the prayer meeting. When Dr. Chafer, the school founder, opened the door and took the check from her hand, he was amazed to find it was for was the exact amount they needed. Then, recognizing the cattleman's name on it, he turned to Dr. Ironside and said, *"Well, Harry, God just sold some of His cows!"*

Whatever God has to do, He will, in order to meet your need. He can solve your problem simply by changing the *elements* in it. Think about that.

First, He can remove time. What normally takes

years, takes only moments when God moves. Listen, "For he will finish the work, and cut it short" (Ro 9:28). God can speed up the natural process of your healing. He can so accelerate your harvest that you'll be sowing with one hand and reaping with the other (Amos 9:13). Time is no obstacle to God!

Second, He can remove lack. God told His people to borrow the silver and gold of the Egyptians and take it with them when they left. Why? Because Pharaoh owed them 400 years of back pay with interest. Think; those, who were willing to be led by God, broke the Spirit of lack and got back everything the enemy had stolen from them and the previous ten generations. What has he stolen from you? God wants to give it back to you!

Third, He can remove the enemy! Listen, "The Egyptians whom you have seen today, ye shall see them no more for ever" (Ex 14:13). "How does God remove the enemy's power?" you ask. By increasing yours! John says, "Greater is he that is in you, than he that is in the world" (1Jn 4:4). Satan could take Jesus to the pinnacle of the temple, but he couldn't push Him off - and he can't push you over the edge either.

Fourth, He can remove doubt! If God could make an ax head float, a donkey talk, and a corpse come out of a grave after four days, then you don't have a problem He can't solve.

The question is, "Believe ye that I am able to do this?"

One of the most amazing answers to prayer I ever heard of concerned a woman who received a telephone call at work saying that her daughter was very ill. She left immediately, stopping at a pharmacy to pick up some medicine on her way. But when she returned to her car, she discovered she'd locked her keys inside.

When she called home, the babysitter told her that her daughter was getting worse and suggested that she find something to open the car door with. After looking around she found a rusty old coat hanger, but she didn't know how to use it. So she bowed her head and said, "Lord, please send somebody to help me."

Within seconds a car pulled up, and a dirty, bearded man wearing torn jeans and a biker's skull-rag on his head jumped out. The woman thought, "Lord, is *this* who you've sent?" When the man asked if he could help, she explained, "My daughter's very ill, and I've got to get home. But I've locked my keys in the car." He walked over to the car, and in less than a minute the door was open. In tears, she hugged him and said, "Thank you, you're a very nice man." He replied, "Lady, I'm not a nice man, I just got out of prison today - I was in for car theft!"

Again, she hugged him, but this time she shouted, *"Thank you Lord, you sent me a professional!"*

3

KILL THE SPIDER!

In a church not far from where I grew up in Belfast, an old elder would rise to his feet every Monday night in the prayer meeting and pray, "Lord, we ask thee to remove the cobwebs from our lives!" This continued for years until one night a lady, who knew him only too well, got up right after him and said, "Lord, just kill the spider!"

When you pray, "Forgive my sins," which ones are you talking about? When you say, "Make me a better person," what *specific areas* would you like Him to work on?

If you want to get real with God, answer these questions:

1. Am I honest and above reproach in all my financial dealings? (That includes giving God His portion.)

2. Do I put myself in sexually inappropriate

situations, or expose myself to harmful material?

3. Do I spend quality time with my family?

4. Do I tell the truth even when it costs me?

5. Do I find it easy to say "I was wrong, I'm genuinely sorry," or do I hold grudges?

6. Am I knowingly compromising any area of my life, or refusing to face the consequences of my actions?

7. Have I formed habits that are detrimental to my health, my job, or my walk with Christ?

8. Am I proud, selfish, or arrogant?

9. Have I taken credit for things that others have done and for which they should have been rewarded?

10. Have I failed to confess my wrongdoing to someone who needs to know about it?

11. Have I been abusive towards my loved ones, and if so, what am I willing to do about it?

12. Am I spending enough time in prayer and in the Scriptures?

Some of us will travel half way round the

world for a personal "word," yet we won't spend one hour alone with God, or deal with the doubt, anger, and selfishness in our hearts. Yet, that's what separates us from Him.

In God's presence you become aware of the condition of your heart. Things that never bothered you before, suddenly, begin to trouble you. Things like words; words that wound others - words that exalt self - words that contradict God.

The first thing the Angel of the Lord did to Isaiah as he stood before the altar, was to take a burning coal and touch his lips saying, "Thine iniquity is taken away and thy sin purged" (Isa 6:7). Do your lips need cleansing today?

And what about your *ways*? Sometimes God removes His discernible presence from us in order to make us reach harder for Him. *Seeking* is what keeps our hearts tender. Without realizing it, we become set in our methods of ministry, set in our ideas about prayer, and set in our attitudes toward others. We take a past experience we've had with

God, reduce it to a formula, and feel like we don't need to seek Him afresh.

Look out; you can seemingly be doing all "the right things," yet your love has grown cold. Listen, "He did what was right in the eyes of the Lord, but not wholeheartedly" (2Ch 25:2 NIV). There it is - your whole heart. Does God have it? Or are you just going through the motions?

Before God could change Jacob He had to get him alone. Listen, "And Jacob was left alone; and there wrestled a man with him until the breaking of the day" (Ge 32:24). When God begins to deal with you, He'll get you alone. He'll wrestle with you until you start to see His purpose for your life and surrender to it.

Sometimes when He deals with us, we try to immerse ourselves in people and activity in an attempt to hide from Him. But it doesn't work. When He performs surgery, He allows nobody in the operating room except the surgeon and the patient!

You see, He's not there to comfort you - that will happen later. He's there to confront you! He wants to talk to you about the *lie* you're living, the *habits* that are destroying your life, and the *mediocrity* you're settling for. He'll wrestle with you until you see the need to keep that job instead of quitting again; or stay in that marriage and not run like you have every other time. He won't sugarcoat the issue; He'll give it to you straight! He'll wrestle with you *until* you're willing to face your situation honestly.

I challenge you today to kneel down and confess your sins to God. Don't ask Him to fix others. Ask Him to fix *you*. It takes courage to do that. But when you do, He'll repair the broken places. All He requires is that you expose them to Him.

4

PASSIONATE PRAYING

There comes a time when you just need to look up and cry out to God from the depths of your being, without worrying about how you look or what others think. Away with superficial, sugar-coated, Sunday-go-to-meeting prayers! Real prayer is not made for human ears. David said, "In my distress I called to the Lord ... From his temple he heard my voice; my cry came before him, into his ears ... He reached down from on high and took hold of me; he drew me out of deep waters. He rescued me from my powerful enemy, from foes, who were too strong for me" (Ps 18:6,16-17 NIV).

Every parent knows that cry. It's different from a temper tantrum or a whining cry for attention. It's a cry of distress, and even though it comes in the dead of night, before you know it your feet are on the floor, and you're at your child's side, holding him, changing him, feeding him, and comforting him.

That's how God feels about *you* today!

Listen, "You will seek me and find me when you seek me with all your heart" (Jer 29:13 NIV). Regardless of how successful you are, there will be times when you need God - and nothing else will do!

This is what the police call an "APB" - an All Points Bulletin. All departments focused on the same thing. It's their top priority. No distractions are permitted.

Often it takes a crisis to produce in us a unified effort; body, soul, and spirit - all points seeking the same thing. God has the answer. He has the blessing waiting for us. But it takes an APB to bring it about.

"But I'm never quite sure how to approach God," you say.

The truth is, there is no "right way" or "only way" to seek Him. It's like lovemaking; it must be personal and spontaneous, conceived out of the power of the moment. You can talk to God walking along a beach, kneeling in church, driving your car, or just lying quietly in bed. Your location and posture are not *half* as important as the hunger that's in your heart.

Songwriter, Ray Palmer, writes: "My faith looks up to thee, Oh Lamb of Calvary." Your faith looks up because your eyes can't see! It's like the natural compensation that occurs when someone is blind, and his *other senses* become keener as a result.

When you press through in prayer, your eyes are suddenly opened, your faith is activated, and you see into a realm where all things are possible.

Nothing fuels real prayer like need. It causes both the gifted and the obscure to cry, "Without You I can do nothing! Indeed, anything I could accomplish without You would mean nothing."

This is the place of *naked prayer*. It's where Hannah was when she cried to God for a child. So passionate was she, that Eli, the High Priest, thought she was drunk (1Sa 1:13). Yet, God heard her cry, and that day Samuel was conceived in her heart. Shortly thereafter he was conceived in her womb.

Refuse to leave the place of prayer until you conceive; until the vision is born; and until the embryo of God's purpose begins to take form within you.

Listen again to David the Psalmist, "As the deer pants for water, so I *long* for you, O God" (Ps 42:1 LB). We don't long for something unless we *value* it and *need* it. Only raw need will cause us to turn away from every other visible means of support and pursue God, because we know that without Him we can't make it. The truth is, if we didn't need Him so desperately, we could easily become satisfied with lesser things.

Three things happen when you pursue God with all of your heart:

1. You step into a realm of the miraculous (Mk 10:27).

2. You grow in character, because you become like the company you keep (2Co 3:18).

3. You learn that certain levels of blessing are never achieved unless you diligently seek God for them (Heb 11:6).

When boils, bankruptcy, and bereavement hit Job's life, he went looking for God. Listen, "Oh that I knew where I might find him!" (Job 23:3). He knew that only in the presence of God would he find the answers he was looking for.

If you've been searching for God, be encouraged; your very search is an act of worship. That's right. When you seek Him, it shows that you value Him. It also says you recognize that He can do for you what nobody else can.

Maybe you wonder today, "Where is the God who breathed life into Ezekiel's *Valley of Dry Bones* and caused them to live again? Where is the Potter who takes broken vessels and puts them back together again? The truth is, He's within touching distance ... hearing distance ... and responding distance. Paul writes that, "He is not far from each one of us" (Acts 17:27 NIV).

The issue is not so much His presence, as it is our *perception* of it. Even His own disciples failed to recognize Him when He came walking towards them on the Sea of Galilee. That's the challenge, isn't it? We wonder, "Is this really God, or is it just my imagination?" We're afraid we'll be disappointed, or even embarrassed, if we trust Him. Jesus calmed their fears by saying, "It is I, don't be afraid" (Mk 6:50 NIV).

Today, He's saying the same thing to you!

5

PRAYING CONFIDENTLY

"So let us come boldly to the throne of our gracious God. There we will receive his mercy, and we will find grace to help us when we need it" (Heb 4:16 NLT).

My friend, Sarah Utterbach, writes, "I'm not shy about praying for anything I need, whether it's in my personal life, or about moving a particular project to the next phase. There are only four possible responses I can get, 'Yes, no, maybe, or not now.' Since I might hear 'Yes,' I have everything to gain and nothing to lose by asking.

"God knows what I need before I ask; yet Jesus said to ask anyway. Why? Because asking God for great things tells Him how big your view of Him is!

"We call ourselves 'humble' when we pray with the mindset of a pauper. Yet God wants us to do great things for Him, and to ask in His name.

Listen, 'Hitherto have ye asked nothing in my name: ask, and ye shall receive, that your joy may be full' (Jn 16:24).

"Stop trying to bring about the purposes of God with mere plans and programs. Nervous breakdown, burnout, or fleecing the sheep, is *never* God's way of getting the job done.

"Ask God for the right kind of help. Sow and expect a harvest. Practice patience. Remind God constantly that you have no agenda; therefore, you're willing to do whatever He wants done as He provides.

"Never quit anything He gives you to do; simply recognize seasons of beginnings, and seasons of endings." What insight!

In Joshua, Chapter 1, we read these words: "Go in to possess the land, which the Lord your God giveth you" (Jos 1:11).

When God says He has given you a certain thing, that means it's yours. But when He says, "Possess it," that means you'll have to *fight* for it, otherwise you'll never receive what He's promised you!

At the moment somebody else may be living in the house you've dreamed of, or holding down the job you believe God has promised to you. But if God says it's yours - stand on it! Instead of shouting about something you're not possessing, get up and go after it!

God says He has given us "All things that pertain unto life" (2Pe 1:3), but you must believe that promise inwardly before you can manifest it outwardly. Often the challenge is to believe in your *spirit* that you're already healed, before you see it actually manifested in your body. Just because something's not evident right now doesn't mean you don't have it.

When you ask God for an oak tree, He gives you an acorn. Now if you don't understand, you might conclude that He either didn't hear your prayer, or that He said no. Not so; the oak tree is already *in* the acorn; it's only a matter of time until it comes out. The seeds of whatever God has promised are already within you. Water them, nurture them, and whatever you do don't let anyone uproot them through unbelief.

If you want to receive anything from God, you've got to do these two things:

First, make up your mind! Reach for what God has promised you. Be tenacious! As long as you're passive and comfortable without it, you won't pursue it.

Second, visualize your victory! Before the building is constructed the architect already has a picture in his mind and a blueprint on his desk. By faith Abraham "saw" his children. He counted them every time he looked at the stars (Ge 15:5). Use your memory to replay past victories, and your imagination to pre-play future ones. That's what David did before he slew Goliath. Look your giant squarely in the face today and declare, "You're coming down, in the name of the Lord!"

The only way Satan can keep you from receiving God's blessings is through deception. Listen, "My people are destroyed for lack of knowledge" (Hos 4:6). When you discover what *really* belongs to you, you'll never be passive again.

Do you remember what Jacob stole from his brother Esau? First, his birthright; that amounted to a double portion of the family inheritance. Second, his blessing; that meant authority to become head of the family. What a loss! Listen to what Isaac said to his son, Esau, "And it shall come to pass when thou shalt have the dominion, that thou shalt break his yoke from off thy neck" (Ge 27:40).

There's a lesson here for you: if you're ever going to *get back* what the enemy has stolen from you, you've got to rise up, use the authority God has given you, and break his hold on your life!

When the Amalekites stole everything that King David held near and dear, including his family, God told him to "Pursue ... overtake ... and recover all" (1Sa 30:8). Today He's saying to you,

"It's time to rise up and take it back!"

In 2 Kings, Chapter 7, we read of a famine that engulfed the city of Samaria, to the extent that people were eating their own children. In the middle of this crisis the prophet Elisha stood up and announced, "By this time tomorrow ... four gallons of barley grain will be sold in the markets of Samaria for one dollar!" But not everybody believed him. Listen again, "The officer assisting the King said, 'That couldn't happen if the Lord made windows in the sky!' But Elisha replied, 'You will see it happen, but you won't be able to buy any of it.'" (2Ki 7:1-2 LB). And he didn't. When the miracle took place, he was trampled under the feet of those running to get what God had provided.

God has wonderful things in store for you but you must *believe* Him, otherwise His blessings will pass you by and go to those who do!

Do you remember the theme song from the musical *Annie*? "Tomorrow, tomorrow, I love you, tomorrow. You're only a day away." If what God has promised you hasn't happened yet, then get excited about tomorrow; for you not only have a past - you also have a future!

The God who says, "... the vision is yet for an appointed time ..." (Hab 2:3), is saying to you right now, "Tomorrow about this time - I'm going to move on your behalf! I know the pressure you're under. I know what others have said. I've seen you standing in faith, and *tomorrow* I'm going to turn this situation around for you, if only you'll believe Me!"

6

PRAYING THE WORD

My mother had an old friend in Northern Ireland, named Beatrice. During the worst of the sectarian violence, when people couldn't get to church because there was no public transportation, a group of believers would meet every week in our home for a Bible study.

One of their favorite passages to study was Psalm, Chapter 91. "He shall cover thee with his feathers, and under his wings shalt thou trust" (verse 14).

One night as Beatrice was walking home from the Bible study, a gang attacked her. As she struggled to keep them from getting her purse, she suddenly remembered Psalm 91, but in her panic she couldn't remember the exact words. So she just stood on the sidewalk and screamed, "Feathers! Feathers! Feathers!"

It worked! The gang thought she was nuts and took to their heels without harming her or getting so much as a penny of her money!

You may smile, but David said, "Thy word have I hid in mine heart" (Ps 119:11). Even if you can't recall the exact words, just keep the concept in your heart, and the God who always honors His Word, will come through for you.

Jesus said, "Whosoever shall *say* unto this mountain, Be thou removed ... and shall not doubt in his heart ... those things which he *saith* ... he shall have whatsoever he *saith*" (Mk 11:23). You'll notice that Jesus referred to what you *believe* once, but what we *say* - three times. Could that be because we already know so much about believing, but so little about how to speak to our situation?

Don't talk *about* your mountain, talk *to* it! Make His Word yours, and the mountain will become your servant. It must, for Jesus said so.

Whether you know it or not, your words are deciding what your tomorrow will be like.

Everything you say either brings you one step closer to what God has promised you or pushes you one step further away from it. Break the habit of negative thinking and doubt-filled words. If God says it, that settles it! He's the *creator* and you're the *creation*; stop arguing with the One who made you!

Dr. Mike Murdock says, "You are the offspring of a perfect God - talk like it! His covenant with you is forever - think like it! Your total well-being is His desire - live like it!"

John the Apostle wrote, "Beloved, I wish above all things that thou mayest prosper and be in health, even as thy soul prospereth" (3Jn:2). Sickness is a thief. It can steal time from those you love. It can steal the money you need to achieve your goals. It can steal the energy required to fulfill God's purpose for your life.

The Bible says that Jesus, "Healed all that were sick: That it might be fulfilled which was spoken by Esaias the prophet, saying, Himself took our

infirmities, and bare our sicknesses'" (Mt 8:16-17).
That means He has *already* purchased everything
required for your well being at the cross; so rise up
in faith and claim it today!

Faith is what qualifies you. It separates you
from those who *need*, and places you among those
who *receive*.

Isaiah writes, "For as the rain and snow come
down from the heavens ... water the earth and *make
it bring forth* ... so shall My word be that goes forth
out of my mouth; it shall not return to me void ...
it shall prosper in the thing for which I sent it"
(Isa 55:10-11 AMP). When you stand on the
Word, speak the Word, and send the Word, you
are helping to "make it bring forth."

Solomon says that the power to bring life or
death to anything lies in your tongue (Pr 18:21).
What you say is an expression of what you believe.

Have you ever seen a dream destroyed by negative words? I have. Have you ever seen a life torn
apart by cruel words? I have. Have you ever seen

faith killed by doubting words? I have. Your words have power!

Listen, "You have *said* ... what have we gained by obeying his commands?" (Mal 3:14 NLT). Have you ever said that? Or have you ever said, "I don't believe in this sowing and reaping stuff; it's just how preachers raise money?" Have you ever said, "I don't believe God heals today?" Look out; you can dig your grave with your tongue!

Just because God promises you something doesn't mean it will automatically happen. No, you must come into *agreement* with the One who "Calls things that are not as though they were" (Ro 4:17 NIV). By doing that, you're not being "flaky," you're just agreeing with God.

God wants you to prosper - believe that! *Prosperity* simply means, "having enough to do the will of God." Do you believe God has a will for your life? Do you believe He wants you to have enough to carry it out? *That's* prosperity!

The Bible says that if you need a financial harvest, sow a financial seed (2Co 9:6). But there's more; you must water your seed by praying and speaking God's Word over it regularly. *That's part of what makes it "bring forth."*

7

PRAYING ACCORDING TO GOD'S WILL

One of my favorite Bible teachers writes, "God has taught me to keep living the life I now have, while I'm waiting for the things that are in my heart to come to pass. We can become so intent on trying to birth the next thing, that we neither enjoy nor take care of the things at hand. I had a vision from God ten years before I began to see it fulfilled. During those years, I believe I missed a lot, by trying to give birth to something outside of God's timing."

Learn to enjoy where you are while you're waiting to get to where you want to be. You see, you'll spend more time in life waiting than you will receiving. Furthermore, when you receive what you're waiting for, you'll immediately begin waiting for something else. That's life. If you don't learn to wait well, you'll live with endless frustration.

Waiting well is what will deliver your dream. Paul says, "And let us not be weary in well doing: for in due season we shall reap, if we faint not" (Gal 6:9). Due season is when God knows you're ready, not when you *think* you're ready.

He has appointed times for accomplishing certain things in your life, so you might as well settle down and wait patiently - for *that's* when they'll happen and not before.

One lady told me, "For years I tried to change my family. But the more I tried, the more they resisted me, and the worse things got. Finally, I began to understand that *people can't change other people - only God can!* I'd been trying to do something I didn't have the power to do. My job was to love them, pray for them, be patient with them, and let God change them. And when I got out of His way, He did!"

You see God doesn't work according to your plans or your timetable. Only when you accept that, will you be *free* from obsessing over people or situations, and be able to commit them to God.

Ask yourself, "If I wasn't trying to control the outcome, what would I be doing differently? What decisions would I be making? What boundaries would I be setting?"

When you try to play God, everybody gets hurt. You get hurt because others can't, or won't, do what you want. They get hurt because your love comes with strings attached. And you're not doing God any favors either.

God said, "I will make darkness light before them, and crooked things straight" (Isa 42:16). Did you hear that? Straightening people out is *God's job* - let Him do it!

But you say, "I don't know how to pray about this, because I'm not sure what God's will is in this matter."

Listen, "He made known to us the mystery of his will" (Eph 1:9 NIV). What a joy it is when the will of God is no longer a mystery, because He makes it known to us. When that happens, our outlook becomes different, and fear can no longer play with our minds. Now we *know* - and knowledge is power!

There are times when we know things in our *spirit* that we can't figure out in our *head*, and it can cause us to be misunderstood. We can carry inside us the knowledge of a breakthrough or a blessing long before it ever happens. Listen, "We know these things because God has revealed them to us by his Spirit" (1Co 2:10 NLT).

What is it that separates the bank president from the janitor? It's what he knows! Both may be equal in every other sense, but one has paid a price to know certain things that set him apart and bring him greater rewards.

God can cause you to *know* something in an instant that will change the rest of your life. He can reveal something to you during the night that will change how you feel about yourself in the morning. In His presence you discover things that give you purpose, hope, dignity, and the strength to get up and fight for what's rightfully yours.

Just because God *has* something doesn't mean He'll automatically *give* it to you. No, a good father uses restraint. He's not only good *to* His children, He's good *for* them. Often He withholds things for a season in order to temper their character and correct their flawed behavior. Then when the blessing comes, they're mature enough to handle it.

If you don't understand that, you can become discouraged and turn away from Him in anger because you believed for something that either didn't come on time, or come at all. But if your faith in God's wisdom is stronger than your personal agenda, you'll hold on to His promise, trust Him, and wait patiently for the answer to come.

It takes maturity to understand that if God doesn't supply it, you don't need it - or don't need it *yet*. If you needed it, He'd give it to you. His Word says, "No good thing will he withhold from them that walk uprightly" (Ps 84:11).

When you're operating in faith, and there's still

a discrepancy between what you *think* you need and what's actually being supplied, remember God knows best; trust Him!

What would it profit you anyway, if you gained the whole world and lost your soul? (Mk 8:36). Don't stress-out or lose-out over material things. Put God's purposes first, and all these *things*, whatever they are, will be yours when the time is right. (Mt 6:33). They may not come when you *want* them, but they will come when you *need* them.

Paul writes, "Don't worry about anything; instead, pray about everything ... If you do this you will experience God's peace" (Php 4:6-7 LB). God's peace; what a wonderful thing to experience! People all around you crave it, but it comes only when you commit your life to Him and operate according to His principles.

When you *commit* something to God, you actually transfer all of it from you to Him. Peter writes, "Casting the whole of your care [all your anxieties, all your worries, all your concerns, once and for all] on Him, for He cares for you" (1Pe 5:7 AMP).

"But how do I cast my cares on Him?" you ask.

By prayer! As soon as you become aware that you're starting to worry or lose your peace of mind, take it to the Lord immediately - and leave it with Him! Don't give the enemy a few days to work you over. The longer you worry, the greater his hold on you will become.

Joyce Meyer says she asked God one day why so many people were struggling with confusion. He replied, *"Tell them to stop trying to figure everything out, and they'll stop being confused!"*

A lot of us need to be delivered from trying to figure everything out. Does that include you? The Bible says, "For God is not the author of confusion" (1Co 14:33). Now, if God is not the author of confusion, then who is? The enemy! He wants to rob you of your peace of mind and keep you confused by getting you to constantly try to figure everything out.

"What can I do?" you ask.

When questions arise, it's okay to ponder them a while. But the moment you feel confused, begin to thank God that *He* has the answer and that you trust Him to show it to you when the time is right. Isaiah says, "Thou wilt keep him in perfect peace, whose mind is stayed on thee: because he trusteth in thee" (Isa 26:3).

The truth is, He can only be your peace when He becomes your constant focus!

8

PRAYING IN AGREEMENT

When you need an answer to prayer, do these two things. *First*, find someone who'll agree with you in prayer. Some situations won't yield to the prayers of one person alone. That's why Jesus said, "If two of you on earth agree about anything you ask for, it will be done for you by my Father in heaven" (Mt 18:19 NIV). Be quick to appreciate a prayer partner when God sends one into your life, for they multiply your impact before the Throne of God and help you to get results.

Next, find a point-of-contact. Your point-of-contact is any instruction God gives you to help activate your faith. It's literally the point at which your *need* comes in contact with His *provision*. For Naaman it was dipping in the River Jordan. For a woman who had hemorrhaged for twelve years and been pronounced incurable by her doctors, it meant touching the hem of Jesus' garment. A lady I know was instantly healed when a handkerchief, that had been anointed with oil and prayed over by her local church, was placed on her body. (See Jas 5:14 and Acts 19:12).

All you need is something to awaken and release your faith!

God alone chooses the method by which He'll work. Jesus rubbed clay in a blind man's eyes, and his sight was restored. He poured water into empty containers, and it came back out as wine. Stop trying to figure Him out and just be humble enough to follow His instructions. If you argue over His methods, you'll never experience His miracles.

"And the Lord said unto Joshua ... take all *the people of war* with thee" (Jos 8:1).

When trouble hits your life, look for *"the people of war."* They're not just strong in faith, they're also strong in fight. They've been tested and tempered. They're trained for battle. They've developed strategies for winning. They've got that tenacious bulldog spirit which rises above every circumstance and says, "If God be for us, who can be against us?" (Ro 8:31).

The people of war are really the people of *the Word*. They know how to take the Sword of the Spirit, which is the Word of God, and use it to defeat the enemy. While others treat their swords as ornaments, or display them in ceremonial parades, *they* know how to march into the enemy's camp and take back everything he has stolen.

Anybody can walk with you in the sunshine or worship with you on Sunday morning, but when you find people who will go to war alongside you, treasure them - they're a gift! Solomon says, "A brother is born for adversity" (Pr 17:17). Did you hear that? *They're born for it!*

You won't always find these people on church platforms, for they blow no trumpet, wave no banner, and demand no applause. But, like battering rams, they know how to break through the gates of hell and procure the promises that belong to us.

Listen again, "Take all the people of war with thee, and arise, go up to Ai: see, I have given into thy hand the king ... and his people ... and his land" (Jos 8:1).

9

THE IMPORTANCE OF PRAISE

Too many of us are like the little boy who, when asked if he said his prayers every night, replied, "No, some nights I don't need anything!"

Prayer is not just about asking, it's about adoring. It's not just about petitioning, it's also about praising. David said, "I will bless the Lord at all times: his praise shall continually be in my mouth. My soul shall make her boast in the Lord: the humble shall hear thereof, and be glad. O magnify the Lord with me, and let us exalt his name together" (Ps 34:1-3).

Please notice three things here:

First, real praise begins as an act of your will. Listen, "I will bless the Lord at all times." It's not an impulse, it's a decision regardless of how you feel or the circumstances you're facing. The word *"hallelujah"* is a command; it's an order to start praising the Lord. Remember that the next time you hear it!

Next, real praise stirs your emotions. Listen, "My soul [emotions] shall make her boast in the Lord." First, David praises the Lord because he's commanded to, and then he does it because he wants to.

Finally, real praise will spread to others. Listen, "O magnify the Lord with me, and let us exalt his name together" (Ps 34:3). It's contagious! Praise will change the climate around you and rub off on others. When you get together with people of praise, decorum will give way to delight, and you'll suddenly find yourself lifted into a new dimension of joy.

The Bible teaches us that there are nine ways to praise the Lord. You can speak, shout, or sing. You can clap your hands, raise them, or play musical instruments. You can stand, kneel, or even dance (Ps 150). With *that* many options, you have no excuse!

When my grandchildren were learning to

walk, I noticed that they'd lift up their hands. I later discovered that this is what gave them *a sense of balance*. What a lesson! Your life will never be balanced if all you do is request things from God but never take the time to praise Him. David says that if you want to reach God, you must enter His gates with thanksgiving, cross His courtyard with praise, and you'll find Him waiting for you there (Ps 100:4).

When those little ones came toddling towards me with their hands up, I couldn't resist! Even if they sometimes didn't smell too good, just one look at those tiny faces and outstretched hands, and I was *compelled* to pick them up, hold them close, and love them!

And it's the same with your Heavenly Father. When you reach up to Him and say, "I love You, I adore You, I need You," He picks you up and carries you through the rough places. He holds you close and whispers, "Fear not ... I have called thee by thy name; thou art mine" (Isa 43:1).

How well do you know God anyway? Do you know that He's not just strong - *He's all-powerful*? That He doesn't just gather information and arrive at conclusions - *He's all knowing*? That He's *omnipresent*, which means wherever you go, *He's there*?

If you can talk about God and feel nothing, you probably don't know Him very well. What is He to you anyway? Your Savior ... your Healer ... your Protector ... your Provider? *The level on which you know Him will determine the level on which you worship Him. Therefore, the passion of your life should be to know Him better. And you can only do that by spending time with Him!*

But be careful; if you seek only His provision but not His presence, you're treating Him like a genie; rub the bottle, out He comes and gives you what you want. That's like witchcraft!

Furthermore, how can you say He's *Lord* of your life yet still fight Him for a dime out of every dollar? (Mal 3:8). Your giving is an act of worship. That's right! When the Jews worshipped God, the sacrifices they laid on the altar went up in smoke. What's my point? Simply this; true worship focuses on what He gets out of it - not what we get!

Praise brought down the walls of Jericho for Joshua. Praise opened prison doors for Paul and Silas. And praise is the package in which we must always present our needs to God. Paul says, "With thanksgiving, present your requests to God" (Php 4:6 NIV).

Sometimes when I'm praying, I simply run out of words. My heart overflows with love, and my lips struggle to find expression. These are the times when I long to *move beyond praise and into the place of intimacy with Him*. Do you ever feel that way? If so, here's a prayer from your heart to His.

"God, you alone are King of my heart; my Hero, my Helper, my Confidant, my Friend. You are the great and only Lover of my soul. My Solace, my Listener, my Amazing One. Protector, Provider, Supreme Sacrificer, Source of life and love and all good gifts.

You are the River that runs through me, the Rock of Ages beneath me, the God of Glory above me, and the Spirit of Life within me.

My heart beats for You. Yours is the love I lean on. Yours is the hand I reach for. Yours is the breast my tears find their way to. You are Counselor, Comforter, and Captain of all my ways.

You are the Searcher of my heart, the Keeper of my secrets, and the Giver of my dreams. You are all the Wonder that is love to me - my most Intimate Companion, and Dweller in the deepest parts of me.

We walk together now, and through all eternity, Savior and sinner, Master and servant, Father and child. The most natural conversation of my day is prayer. The constant beat of my heart is praise. I will love You, Oh Lord, my strength! Amen."

I would like to leave with you some prayers that I believe will help you express your heart to God. Wrap them in faith! Lift them up in praise! Present them to the One who promised, "If ye abide in me, and my words abide in you, ye shall ask what ye will, and it shall be done unto you" (Jn 15:7).

WHEN YOU NEED HEALING

"For I will restore health unto thee, and I will heal thee of thy wounds, saith the Lord." Jeremiah 30:17

Lord, Your Word says that nothing is too difficult for You (Jer 32:17). In Your eyes all sickness is alike, and all of it must bow before You.

I read in Your Word that by Your stripes I am healed (Isa 53:5). You healed a woman, whom doctors pronounced incurable, because she touched the hem of Your garment (Mt 9:20). Make Your presence so real to me, that I too will be able to touch You and be made whole.

You promised Your people that You would take away sickness from the midst of them, and they would live a full and blessed life (Ex 23:25-26). Take this sickness away! Raise me up so that I can fulfill every plan You have for me.

Remove from me any doubt that You are either able or willing to heal. Give me faith, because faith comes from You (Ro 10:17).

Today I claim Your promise, and I declare that I will not die, but live and proclaim what the Lord has done for me (Ps 118:17). In Christ's name. AMEN.

WHEN YOU'RE STRUGGLING TO UNDERSTAND YOUR DESTINY

"I will instruct thee and teach thee in the way which thou shalt go; I will guide thee with mine eye."

Psalm 32:8

Father, I know You have a special destiny for me; that there is more *of* You, and more *from* You than I have right now. You've given me certain gifts, but I can't seem to get them to the place where they can do some good. So here I am, crying, "Lord, what wilt thou have me to do" (Acts 9:6).

I've struggled until I'm finally ready to give You *all* there is of me. Here I am on Your altar, trying to figure out what You want me to do and where You want me to go.

I know that there's an altar-time; a time of consecration beyond readiness; a time to enjoy Your presence without instruction; a time to be made strong so that I can fulfill Your purposes.

Remind me Lord that this consecrating hour is

a priceless moment for You and me - a moment that may never be repeated again. When the consecration is complete, the action begins. But to act well, I must first know the secret of living in Your presence, the secret of receiving strategies from Your Word, and the secret of being moved by the impulse of Your Spirit.

Today, I give myself unreservedly to You. Prepare me *now* for what You have for me *then*. In Christ's name. AMEN.

WHEN YOU'VE BEEN
SEPARATED OR DIVORCED

"He which hath begun a good work in you will perform it until the day of Jesus Christ." Philippians 1:6

Father, it's no wonder You say You hate divorce (Mal 2:16 NIV). The pain of this is tearing me apart.

Today I confess my sin and take responsibility for my failure in this marriage. Please forgive me and cleanse me.

As I walk through this valley I know You are with me, encouraging me when I feel discouraged, and giving me the strength to go on. Thank You for never giving up on me.

Heal my broken heart. Use this experience to mature me. Soften the rough edges in me that hinder true intimacy with another. Rebuild the remnants of my shattered self-worth. Reestablish my identity, not on what I may have done, or what has been done to me, but only on *who I am according to Your Word.*

I refuse to carry bitterness and unforgiveness. What You endured on the cross for my sins was greater than any pain I have known, yet You forgave. So I choose to forgive, as You have forgiven me.

Keep me from rushing into another relationship in an attempt to fill an emptiness that only *You* can fill. Help me to use the lessons I'm learning each day, to bring healing and wholeness to those who hurt as I do.

God, you can turn beauty into ashes, so turn this situation around for my good and Your glory. In Christ's name. AMEN.

WHEN YOU FACE AN IMPOSSIBLE SITUATION

"The Lord is good, a strong hold in the day of trouble; and he knoweth them that trust him."   Nahum 1:7

Lord, you see where I am right now. I'm not even sure how I got here, and at the moment I can see no way out.

Come and bring Your presence into this situation. Bring the kind of wisdom and encouragement that only *You* can provide. Help me to think big and not limit You. Help me to be sensitive to Your voice; to trust You beyond my fears!

God of fire-by-night and cloud-by-day, get me through this wilderness! God of Joshua, bring down these walls! God of Daniel, shut the mouths of those who seek to destroy me! Master of Galilee, speak peace to this storm, for You are the same yesterday, today, and forever, and Your Word says that there is *nothing* too hard for You. (Jer 32:17).

You created something out of nothing, and

You did it with just a word. Speak now on my behalf, and I know that all will be well. In Christ's name. AMEN.

WHEN YOU LONG TO HAVE CHILDREN

"Now Isaac pleaded with the Lord for his wife, because she was barren; and the Lord granted his plea, and Rebecca his wife conceived."　　Genesis 25:21 NKJV

Father, You created us to be Your children so that You would have someone to love. Today, I come to You in my pain and frustration, asking You for a child that I can pour my love upon as well.

You said that children are a heritage from You, and the fruit of the womb is Your reward (Ps 127:3). Give me this heritage! Make me fruitful! Turn this discouragement into a faith that refuses to give up. Heal this heart that has been broken by endless disappointments.

Just as Isaac pleaded with You for his wife, and she conceived, so I plead with You today to bring healing and life to our bodies, so that we too can conceive.

As I wait on You, nurture in me a sense of self-esteem that is independent of my ability to have children, for my identity and worth don't come from having children, but from the fact that I am *Your* child.

Your Word says that if I delight myself in You, You will give me the desires of my heart (Ps 37:4). Come now and fulfill this desire, for I believe that it is born of You. In Christ's name. AMEN.

WHEN IT'S HARD TO FORGIVE

"Be ye kind...forgiving one another, even as God for Christ's sake hath forgiven you."　　　Ephesians 4:32

Lord, there's nothing harder than trying to forgive when you've been badly wounded. And it's worse when the offenders seem to show no remorse, and even gloat over the pain they've brought into your life. That's where I am today, and I don't want to forgive.

I know enough to understand that I must - no matter what, for You have given me no option. But I'm struggling with it.

I know that unforgiveness can kill; it can destroy my friendships, my joy, my peace, and my potential; that's a price I'm not prepared to pay. So today I *choose* to forgive this one who has taken so much from me; who has broken my heart and wounded me.

Thank You Lord for the strength to walk in love, especially when the memories return, and "the committee" in my head begins to speak. Thank You for the grace to forgive moment by moment, as You have forgiven me. In Christ's name. AMEN.

FOR THE SALVATION
OF AN UNSAVED LOVED ONE

"The Lord is ... patient ... not wanting anyone to perish, but everyone to come to repentance."

2 Peter 3:9 NIV

Father, I know that what I'm asking is in accordance with Your will because You have said You want "All men to be saved, and to come to a knowledge of the truth" (1Ti 2:4 NIV).

You care for my loved ones more than I do, and when You were hanging on the cross, You were thinking not only of me, but of them too.

In the name of Jesus, I bind the powers of darkness that would hinder them from coming to You! (Mt 16:19). Close their eyes to deception. Shut their ears to every lie the enemy tells them. Whatever it takes, bring them to the place of complete submission to You.

I know there is nothing I can do to change them - but You can! Open their heart to the truth of Your Word (Ps 119:18). Bring people into their path who will point them to You and share with them Your Word.

Show me my role in Your redemptive process. Help me to say and do nothing that would hinder Your Spirit's work.

Your Word says that if we ask anything according to your will, You will do it (1Jn 5:14-15). Today, I claim my loved ones for You. In Christ's name. Amen.

WHEN THINGS FALL APART

"The Lord is my strength and my shield; my heart trusts in him and I am helped."   Psalm 28:7 NIV

Lord, I can't believe how suddenly things can change, and how completely. Just moments ago my life seemed happy and secure. Now it feels like I've stepped on a land mine, and my world is shattered.

Right now I'm not even sure *what* I need from You, or how to pray about this situation. So I rest in the promise that You know my every need and You will provide for me.

Send Your Holy Spirit to bring truth, bring deliverance, and bring understanding as to what I need to do next.

As I said, I have nothing left but You. But You are all I need. You are my Rock, and my Sure Foundation. Thank You for being there. I leave it all in Your capable hands today, confident that You will work it out. In Christ's name. AMEN.

WHEN YOU CAN'T SLEEP

"He gives his beloved sleep." Psalm 127:2

Lord, this fatigue is affecting everything I do; my work, my emotions, my relationships, and even my walk with You. More than just sleep, I need that special rest which comes from You.

Your Word says that You give sleep to those You love. Give it to me now, for my body is tired and my soul is weary. Lift me out of fear, distraction, and restlessness, and into the place of quiet repose. Keep my mind in perfect peace, because my thoughts are constantly focused on You.

Your Word says that You neither slumber nor sleep, so there's no need for me to stay awake too. Help me now to cast all my concerns on You, knowing that all will be well, for nothing can reach me, that does not first pass by You.

Your Word says You have not given me the spirit of fear (2Ti 1:7). So right now, I rebuke every fear, cast down every imagination, and take every thought captive (2Co 10:5).

I declare with the Psalmist, "I will both lie down in peace, and sleep; for you alone, O Lord, make me dwell in safety" (Ps 4:8 NKJV). In Christ's name. AMEN.

WHEN YOU FEEL DISCOURAGED

"Do not throw away your confidence; it will be richly rewarded."　　　　　Hebrews 10:35 NIV

Lord, I've done everything I know to see my dreams come true. I've had seasons of working hard and seasons "of letting go and letting God." Still, the things I've believed for, seem like they'll never happen.

I feel like Sarah - like I'll never hold the one thing I long for most. God, don't let me miss my destiny. Don't let me hope for things that are not part of Your plan for my life. Let me hear Your voice guiding me, reassuring me, and telling me You love me.

Remind me again of Your promise to me, so that I can fight with faith, and take hold of it. Help me also to understand the difference between what I must go after, and what I must wait on You for. When it's up to me, give me the strength to march fearlessly into the new day You've prepared for me. When it's up to You, give me grace and patience to wait; fill me with the joyful anticipation that accompanies a perfectly timed present.

Lord, they say that You are never, ever late. In these days of waiting, keep me firm in my faith. Don't let me stop short of my blessing. Remind me again that I must not throw away my confidence, for it will be richly rewarded! In Christ's name. AMEN.

WHEN YOU'RE IN FINANCIAL DISTRESS

"But my God shall supply all your needs according to his riches in glory by Christ Jesus." Philippians 4:19

Lord, You know how strapped I am. There is no way out of the situation without Your help. It seems like every time I pick up the phone or open the mail, it's another bill collector. Not only am I out of money, I'm out of patience, hope and ideas. I never realized how important money was to me, until I spent more than I had. Now I'm trapped in a cycle of debt, that is out of control.

Your Word says You will "supply all my need," so I am calling on You today to be my Supplier. I repent of unwise spending choices I have made. I repent of the lack of discipline that got me into this mess. Please work a miracle in my finances. Give me creative ways to make money, and the wisdom to know how to use it.

I commit to walk with You, Lord, until I "owe

no one anything except love" (Ro 13:8). Thank you, Lord, for Your promise of provision and release. In Christ's name. AMEN.

WHEN YOU'VE LOST
THE ONE YOU LOVE

"As a mother comforts her child, so I will comfort you."
Isaiah 66:13 NIV

Lord, my heart hurts with a pain I've never known before! Today I need hope, and I need help. Well-meaning people come with words of kindness, but their love cannot reach the depths of my soul, where there's so much pain.

I feel lost and alone at this moment. Death ended what we had together, and what we were together - one flesh, one mind, one spirit.

Father I need You; I don't want to face the world by myself! Pull me back from the grave of my grief. Soften the pain I feel when everything I see, reminds me of them.

Deliver me from feeling guilty over the things I wish had been different between us. Help me to realize that they understood the things we both should have said more often.

You said, "As a mother comforts her child, so I will comfort you." Send Your comfort, for You are the only One who understands where I am right now, and I'm leaning on You.

Bring the light of Your presence to this dark place I'm in. Restore me with the tenderness of Your mercy, until I'm strong and whole again. Thank You for being by my side, every moment of this day. In Christ's name. AMEN.

WHEN A MARRIAGE IS DIFFICULT.

"Live a life of love, just as Christ loved us and gave himself up for us."   Ephesians 5:2 NIV

Lord, how can something that started so fresh, now seem so stale? The intimacy has gone. Our love has lost its spontaneity; it all feels so cold and canned. Please break through this veil of politeness that hides our hushed frustration and despair. Do something!

Give me the grace to forgive, when I face insensitivity; teach me, because I don't always know how. Help me to realize that I'll always have to love an imperfect person - and so will they.

Today I'm learning so much about Your unconditional love for me, as I try to reach out to one who's so out of touch with where I am.

You are the Potter, and we are the clay. Take this relationship that seems so marred and make it over again. Fashion us for each other. Breathe life into it. Allow us to be friends once more: to love, to laugh, and to play together, for I miss the way it used to be.

Thank you for knowing what to do with our hearts. Today I declare by faith that there will be a change because of You. In Christ's name. AMEN.

ABOUT THE AUTHOR

Bob Gass was born in Belfast, Northern Ireland on January 15, 1944. His grandfather was one of the builders of the Titanic.

At 12, he committed his life to Christ, and at 13 he preached his first sermon. Five years later he arrived in America with two sermons in a brief case, twenty-five cents in his pocket, and a burning desire to preach Christ.

For 12 years, he and his older brother, Neil, built and pastored one of the largest churches in northern New England. From 1981 to 1986, Bob hosted his own daily television talk show in Atlanta, Georgia - *The Breakfast Club*.

Twelve years ago, he became a director of United Christian Broadcasters, a missionary organization which has built over 160 Christian radio stations in such places as Russia, Estonia, Ireland, New Zealand, Australia and Europe.

During the last eight years, Bob has taken 40 trips to Romania and Moldova to bring aid to thousands of desperately needy children and elderly people.

He wrote the first edition of *The Word For You Today* seven years ago (3,000 copies). It's now read daily by over one million people, in 19 different languages.

Bob Gass is in great demand as a speaker at conferences and churches around the world. Those who hear him describe him as a gifted orator whose sermons are uplifting, often humorous, and always solution oriented. Many of his messages are available on video and audiocassette. *(Free product catalogue available upon request)*.

Bob's wife, Debby, was also born in Belfast, Northern Ireland. They now make their home in Roswell, Georgia.

To Contact the Author Write:

Bob Gass
P.O. Box 767550
Roswell, GA 30076 USA

Or call: 678-461-9989
Email: TWFYT@wordforyou.com
Visit our web site at: www.wordforyou.com

Personal Notes

PERSONAL NOTES

PERSONAL NOTES

_____

_____

_____

_____

_____

_____

_____

_____

_____

_____

_____

_____

_____

_____

_____

_____

_____

_____

_____

_____

_____

PERSONAL NOTES

_____

_____

_____

_____

_____

_____

_____

_____

_____

_____

_____

_____

_____

_____

_____

_____

_____

_____

_____

_____